All-Star Players™

MEET ELI MANNING

Football's Unstoppable Quarterback

Sloan MacRae

PowerKiDS press
New York

B
Man
12/09

Published in 2009 by The Rosen Publishing Group, Inc.
29 East 21st Street, New York, NY 10010

First Edition

Editor: Amelie von Zumbusch
Book Design: Greg Tucker
Photo Researcher: Jessica Gerweck

Photo Credits: Cover, pp. 4, 8, 9, 10, 11, 12, 14, 15, 17, 18, 19, 20, 21, 25, 27, 29 © Getty Images; p. 7 © FilmMagic; p. 23 © AFP/Getty Images; p. 26 © Associated Press.

Library of Congress Cataloging-in-Publication Data

MacRae, Sloan.
    Meet Eli Manning : football's unstoppable quarterback / Sloan MacRae. — 1st ed.
        p. cm. — (All-star players)
    Includes index.
    ISBN 978-1-4358-2705-9 (library binding) — ISBN 978-1-4358-3097-4 (pbk.)
ISBN 978-1-4358-3103-2 (6-pack)
    1. Manning, Eli, 1981– —Juvenile literature. 2. Football players—United States—Biography—Juvenile literature. 3. Quarterbacks (Football)—United States—Biography—Juvenile literature. I. Title.
    GV939.M289M33 2009
    796.332092—dc22
    [B]
                                                                        2008020332

Manufactured in the United States of America

Contents

Manning wears the number 10 on his uniform. He has worn the same number since he played in college.

The Manning Family Business

Eli Manning is a quiet, but very talented, **quarterback** for the New York Giants. Manning comes from a family of football stars. His father, Archie, was one of the greatest quarterbacks in college football history. Archie also played in the National Football League, or NFL. Eli Manning's older brother Peyton is an even bigger star than Archie. Peyton plays in the NFL for the Indianapolis Colts. Some **experts** think he is the best quarterback ever to throw a football.

Eli Manning is following in his family's footsteps. Talk about pressure! Eli can handle the pressure, though. He is becoming a football **sensation** in his own right.

All-Star Facts

Eli Manning's full name is Elisha Nelson Manning.

Eli Manning was born in New Orleans, Louisiana. He has two older brothers, named Cooper and Peyton. Both of Eli's brothers are several years older than him. When Eli was growing up, Archie was often traveling with his football team. Therefore, Eli and his mother, Olivia, became very close. They spent lots of their time collecting **antiques**. Eli was shy and quiet when he was young. He was also easygoing. In fact, his friends nicknamed him "Easy."

Archie did not pressure his sons to play football, but all three of the Manning brothers loved the sport. Cooper's football dreams ended

All-Star Facts

Eli had trouble reading as a child. However, he worked hard and, in time, became a good student.

Eli still takes part in many activities with his parents and brothers. In 2008, Eli (right), Peyton (left), and their father hosted the NERF Father's Day Football Throwdown, in New York City.

Eli is close to his brothers. Cooper (right) proudly hugged his youngest brother after Eli (left) played a great game.

when he learned about a condition in his spine that made it unsafe for him to play football.

It did not take long for the Manning football talent to rub off on young Eli. He became the star quarterback of his high-school team. Soon the coaches and **scouts** from college football teams began to take an interest in him. They were hoping he had the family talent.

Ole Miss

Manning decided to follow in his father's footsteps and play for the University of Mississippi Rebels. The University of Mississippi is also known as Ole Miss. It is one of the biggest football schools in the country.

Archie Manning is an Ole Miss hero to this day. In fact, the speed limit on the Ole Miss campus, or grounds, is 18 miles per hour (29 km/h) because

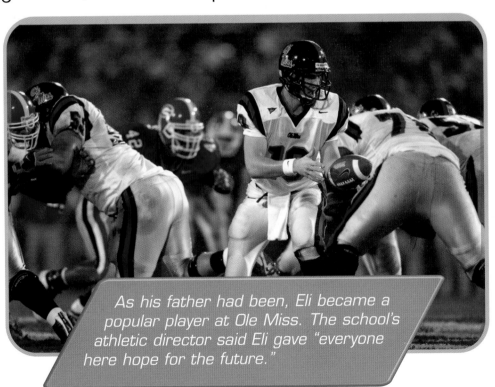

As his father had been, Eli became a popular player at Ole Miss. The school's athletic director said Eli gave "everyone here hope for the future."

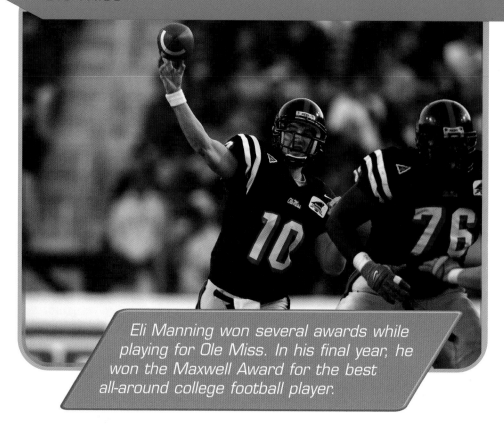

Eli Manning won several awards while playing for Ole Miss. In his final year, he won the Maxwell Award for the best all-around college football player.

Archie wore number 18. The expectations placed on Archie's son were high, and Eli met them. He became the leader of his team with the same easygoing attitude that his family loved.

Just like his father, Eli Manning became an Ole Miss hero. He set or tied 45 different school records. He also studied hard and got excellent grades. Eli even won the National Football Foundation National Scholar-**Athlete** Award. He graduated with honors and earned a **degree** in marketing.

Eli was finished with college, but he was not finished with football. He was ready to play in the NFL!

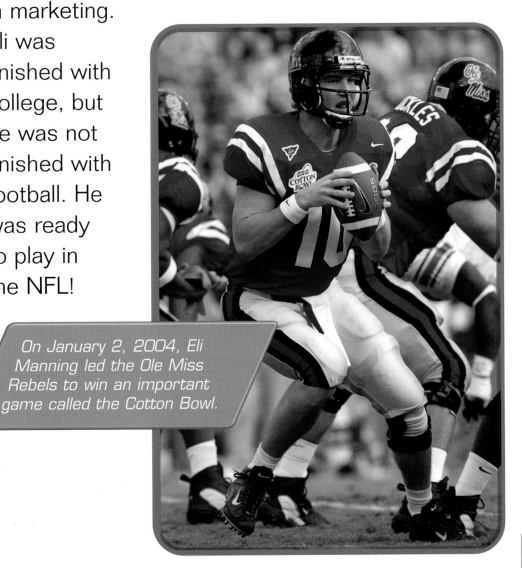

On January 2, 2004, Eli Manning led the Ole Miss Rebels to win an important game called the Cotton Bowl.

Eli Manning was very happy to learn that he had been traded to the Giants on the day of the draft.

The NFL holds a draft every year. In the draft, all 32 NFL teams take turns picking the best young college players. Players selected during the first round of the draft are expected to be **potential** stars. The San Diego Chargers had the first selection in the first round, and they chose Manning. This means that Manning was chosen first out of the 255 players. The Chargers picked Manning, but they did not keep him. Just a few minutes later, they traded him to the New York Giants.

Manning began his first season as one of the Giants' backup quarterbacks. New York already had a starting quarterback, named Kurt Warner.

All-Star Facts

Archie, Peyton, and Eli were all first-round picks in the NFL draft. No other family had ever had three first-round draft picks.

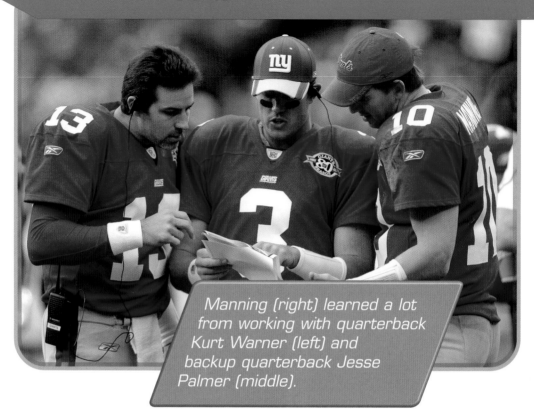

Manning (right) learned a lot from working with quarterback Kurt Warner (left) and backup quarterback Jesse Palmer (middle).

Manning learned a lot by watching Warner lead the team. Later in the season, Manning became the starting quarterback.

Meanwhile, Peyton Manning was enjoying one of his best seasons yet. Football fans, experts, and journalists watched to see how Eli would compare to his big brother. Eli struggled. Fans and sportswriters thought that he looked confused. He did not make Giants fans happy until the very last game of the season, when he finally led his team to victory against the Dallas Cowboys. However, Eli finished his first Giants season with a losing record.

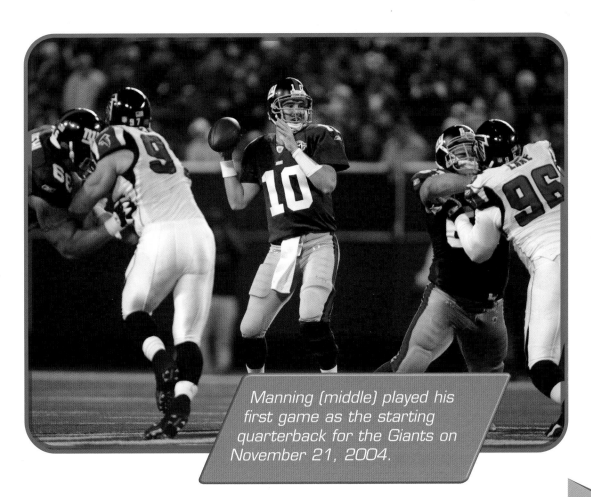

Manning (middle) played his first game as the starting quarterback for the Giants on November 21, 2004.

Eli Manning continued to struggle over the next two years. Fans and journalists expected him to be a star just because his last name was Manning. Sometimes he played well, but other days he was terrible. This **inconsistency** angered the fans. They booed him and said very mean things about him. Star Giants players like Tiki Barber and Jeremy Shockey openly questioned his leadership and even **criticized** him to the **media**.

To make matters tougher, Peyton kept playing astonishing football. Eli found himself in his big brother's shadow. One sportswriter even joked that Eli must be adopted. The fans just got angrier and nastier. Eli Manning refused to let the fans bother him, though. He kept his cool and worked hard to become a better player.

One bright moment in the 2005 season was the game in which the Giants beat the Cowboys, 17–10, on December 4, 2005.

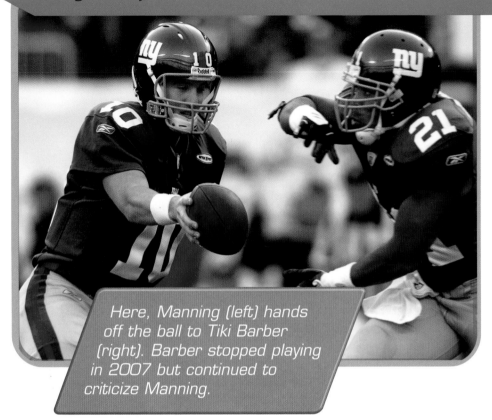

Here, Manning (left) hands off the ball to Tiki Barber (right). Barber stopped playing in 2007 but continued to criticize Manning.

The 2006 season began with one of the biggest opening games in NFL history. Eli and the Giants played Peyton and the Colts. This was the first time that two brothers played starting quarterback for opposing teams. Eli played well, but the Colts proved too much for the Giants. Once again, Eli's season had ups and downs. The Giants lost to the

Philadelphia Eagles in the **postseason**. Peyton and the Colts, however, went on to win the **Super Bowl**. It looked as if Eli would always be in Peyton's shadow.

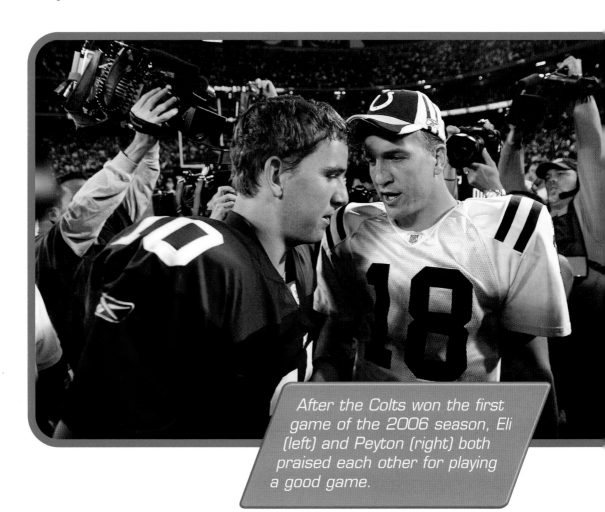

After the Colts won the first game of the 2006 season, Eli (left) and Peyton (right) both praised each other for playing a good game.

On January 20, 2008, the Giants beat the Green Bay Packers and won a spot in the Super Bowl. The game went into overtime and was played in the bitter cold.

Eli the Underdog

The Giants had a wonderful season in 2007 and even reached the Super Bowl! Unfortunately, most football experts paid little attention. They were too busy talking about the New England Patriots. The Patriots needed to win the Super Bowl in order to complete a perfect 19-0 season. This would make

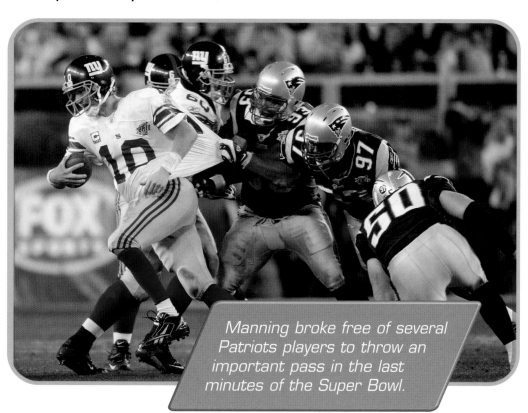

Manning broke free of several Patriots players to throw an important pass in the last minutes of the Super Bowl.

them the best team in football history. Almost nobody thought the Giants could beat the Patriots. However, Eli Manning did not mind playing the part of the underdog. He had been the underdog to his brother since he joined the NFL.

The Super Bowl was a close game. The Giants were losing in the fourth quarter with under 3 minutes left in the game. Manning had one last chance to lead his team. In the most famous play of the game, Manning avoided several sacks and threw a long pass to David Tyree. Soon after, Manning helped win the game by throwing a touchdown pass to Plaxico Burress.

The Giants shocked the football world and beat the Patriots in one of the biggest upsets in sports

All-Star Facts

Eli and Peyton Manning are the only pair of brothers to be named Super Bowl MVPs. They were named MVP in back-to-back years!

history. Manning was named the game's Most Valuable Player, or MVP. He had finally moved out of Peyton's shadow and silenced his critics!

After the Giants won the Super Bowl, Manning proudly held the Vince Lombardi Trophy. This award is given each year to the winner of the Super Bowl.

Manning off the Field

Some journalists have noticed that Manning does not behave like the average **celebrity**. He does not date supermodels. In 2008, he married his college sweetheart, Abby McGrew, at a private service on a beach in Mexico. Manning lives a quiet life.

Manning has many interests aside from football. He enjoys shopping for antiques with his mom and his wife. One of the things Manning cares about most is helping people. In 2005, **Hurricane** Katrina destroyed large parts of the southern United States. Manning's hometown of New Orleans flooded. Many people died, and many more were left homeless. Eli and his brother Peyton worked hard to bring food and supplies to homeless and hungry families. Eli also works with **charities** like the March

Eli Manning and his wife, Abby, enjoy
spending quiet time together at home.
Abby grew up in Nashville, Tennessee.

Eli Manning has worked with the Katrina Krewe, a group that formed to help clean up the trash in the streets of New Orleans after Hurricane Katrina.

of Dimes and the Red Cross to help children with illnesses. Manning has even promised to raise $2.5 million to create the Eli Manning Children's **Clinics** at the University of Mississippi Medical Center.

Family is also important to Manning. He spends as much time with Archie, Olivia, Cooper, and Peyton as he can. In fact, Eli works with Archie and Peyton to run an organization called the Manning Passing Academy. Every summer, the Mannings gather some of the country's best coaches and athletes to help high-school football players improve their skills.

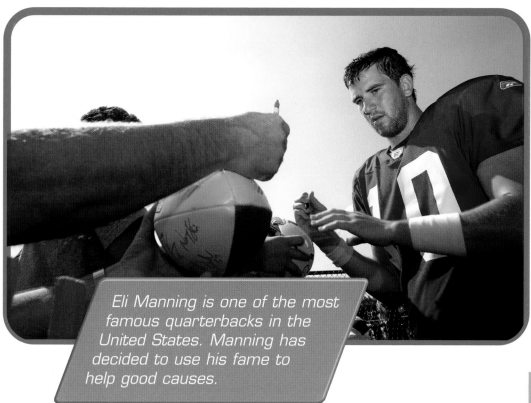

Eli Manning is one of the most famous quarterbacks in the United States. Manning has decided to use his fame to help good causes.

A Guy Called Easy

Eli Manning is still sometimes known by his childhood nickname, Easy. However, his Giants teammates all know that his easygoing nature does not mean Manning lacks **passion**. He has worked hard to prove that he is just as talented as the rest of his family. Manning continues to work hard in order to become an even better player.

Manning already holds football's most important title. Most NFL players never get the chance to win a Super Bowl. It took Peyton 10 years to get there. However, Eli was the star of the Super Bowl in just his fourth season! There is no limit to what Eli Manning can achieve with his hard work and his calm personality.

In his years as a Giant, quiet Eli Manning has become a team leader. He is likely to lead the Giants for many years to come.

Height: 6' 4" (1.9 m)
Weight: 225 pounds (102 kg)
Team: New York Giants
Position: Quarterback
Uniform Number: 10
Date of Birth: January 3, 1981

2007 Season Stats

Passing Yards	Passing Completions	Passing Touchdowns	Quarterback Rating
3,336	297	23	73.9

Career Stats as of 2007 Season

Passing Yards	Passing Completions	Passing Touchdowns	Quarterback Rating
11,385	987	77	73.4

Glossary

antiques (an-TEEKS) Works of art or pieces of furniture made a long time ago.

athlete (ATH-leet) Someone who takes part in sports.

celebrity (seh-LEH-breh-tee) A famous person.

charities (CHER-uh-teez) Groups that give help to the needy.

clinics (KLIH-niks) Places where people can get medical care.

criticized (KRIH-tuh-syzd) Found fault with.

degree (dih-GREE) A title given to a person who has finished a course of study.

experts (EK-sperts) People who know a lot about a subject.

hurricane (HUR-ih-kayn) A storm with strong winds and heavy rain.

inconsistency (in-kun-SIS-tent-see) Not able to be depended on.

media (MEE-dee-uh) Reporters and people who appear on TV and radio shows.

passion (PA-shun) A very strong feeling.

postseason (pohst-SEE-zun) Games played after the regular season.

potential (poh-TEN-shul) Promising.

quarterback (KWAHR-ter-bak) A football player who directs a team's plays.

scouts (SKOWTS) People who help sports teams find new, young players.

sensation (sen-SAY-shun) Something or someone that is very good or exciting.

Super Bowl (SOO-per BOHL) The championship game of NFL football.

Index

Web Sites

Due to the changing nature of Internet links, PowerKids Press has developed an online list of Web sites related to the subject of this book. This site is updated regularly. Please use this link to access the list:
www.powerkidslinks.com/asp/elim/